The D.E.W.
Divine Essential Words Journal

Miriam Whitehead

Broad Wing Press
Lanham, MD

Copyright © Miriam Whitehead

All rights reserved. No parts of this book may be reproduced in any form without written permission from Broad Wing Publications.

Unless otherwise noted, Scripture is taken from the Holy Bible, New King James Version® New International Version®. Copyright© 1982 by Thomas Nelson, Inc. Used by permission. All rights reserved.

Printed in the United States of America

ISBN: 978-1-938373-61-9
LCCN: 2022935096

This is dedicated to those who desire that personal fitting relationship with Jesus without compromise. This is for those who won't feed into the carnal complications which inhibits the plan of salvation. Let the world say that you are strange and peculiar because, at the end of the day it's still "Yea or Nay!"

Miriam Whitehead

Table of Contents

Shelter 1
Where Do Your Words Lie? 3
What's Your Label? 5
Are You In or Of ? 7
The Message In the Wilderness 8
Grateful Moments 9
Capacities 10
Letting Go For Life 11
Positioning For Purpose 12
Complacency 13
Continued Faith 14
Strongholds 15
On Your Mark, Get Set, Stand! 17
Submit 19
Affordable Comfort 21
Parental Rights 23
Spiritual Boomerang 25
A You're Excused Moment 26
No Substitutions 27
The Herd Hears 29
Laboring The Birth 31
Contact 32
Acceptable Rejects 33
Necessary Demonstrations 34
It's In The Presentation 35
The Well In The Desert 36
Greetings 37
My Comings and Goings 38
Case Dismissed 39
The Skin We're In 40
No Returns and No Refunds 41
Expectable 42
And Then There Were None 43
Moments of Sunshine And Rainy Days 45
The Message, The Messenger, and The Messiah 47
What's In A home? 49
The Light In The Lighthouse 50
The Fork In The Road 51
The Off Switch 52
Stakeholders 53
Essions/Distractions 54

Are We There Yet?	55
Skipping Steps	56
Against All Odds	57
Flammable	58
Live	59
The Message You Heard vs. The Message You Speak	60
Do You See What He Said?	61
Disclaimers Disclosures, Dishonest	62
Amen Corners	63
Check Your Punctuation Marks	65
Who Are You?	67
Accountability	69
Pro's and Con's	71

Introduction

In the early part of the mornings, dew is upon the grass as an after moisture. When you wake in the morning your mouth can feel dry, your lips chapped, your skin crying for moisture and then you pause. Right then and just now you realize that water is the only rescue that will quench the places on your body.

During the war above your body in the last shade of night a dryness was produced. Without you knowing it, battles for you soul were going on. In God's omnipresent power he provided a moisture to combat the dry, thirsty, desiccated, and parched areas in your soul. All you had to do was get up in obedience and move in your purpose. God gets the glory. Those droplets of the living water was all your soul needed to start in a refreshing day. The new breath provided at 12:01 midnight, should inspire new hope, now faith, and a willingness to go on.

Let the D. E. W. intertwine in your daily life. This is a check-up and check-out on you and your relationship with Jesus. In all thy ways acknowledge him, and he shall direct thy paths (Proverbs 3:6).

Shelter

My shelter consists of a hovering that casts out light. I'm content with it hiding my inconsistencies and concealing my known tendencies. My shelter shadows my verbal thoughts while I yearn and ache for unwarranted wants. My shelter covers my cowering heart as I seek day. It is to dark and I can't find me. Lord have Thine own way.

What is your shelter covering?

_____
_____
_____
_____

For thou hast been a shelter for me, and a strong tower from the enemy (Ps 61:3)

His shelter reveals the courage embedded in my soul that defies and overwhelms the particulates of my physical stature. Jesus, mature my every move as you contemplate my rebellious human nature. You are forever with me during the shades of the third watch. You illuminate the path and enhance the truth in my walk while clearing the clutter. My steps become strides of purpose. Your shelter is the perfect covering of redeeming light that pierces the darkness without a fight. Thank you for endowing me with armor to withstand the storm and for consistently whispering into my soul the instructions to stand firm. I'm grateful for the inner man that lifts the outer man and defies the law of gravity. I appreciate you, Lord, for stripping away my irregularities while clarifying my spiritual prosperity.

What does His Shelter do in your life?

_____
_____
_____
_____

He sheltered the status of my homeless mind causing my unstable foundations to be redirected to solid ground.

_____
_____
_____
_____

Where Do Your Words Lie?

I'm asking this question, because at times we frustrate ourselves talking out of turn. For example: Constantly telling someone that their friend is not for them can endanger your relationship with that person. Until God reveals it to them, you're just driving your own self crazy. Just because He revealed it to you doesn't always mean time to tell. As parents, we find ourselves talking to our adult children about what they should be doing, and when are they going to get it right etc... They perceive it as fussing and they think you're trying to control them. Just saying "hello and how are you" can go a long way. Slipping into judging our children or others is not our place (I know you want to call it parenting). After all that talking, did it fall on deaf ears? Quarreling or yelling doesn't work, but prayer does.

I spoke out of turn when... So now I will...

_____
_____
_____
_____

Give not that which is holy unto the dogs, neither cast ye your pearls before swine, lest they trample them under their feet, and turn again and rend you (Matt 7:6)

Christians, in our daily routine, ministering and spreading the gospel are strategic maneuvers. This is to be in the mindset of glorification unto God and not edification for you. Is what you're saying laying on the hearts of men for condemnation or for the repentance of sin? Is it to help with their relationship with Jesus, or "hearken unto you because of, you?" In chess the knight can be used for checkmate. Moving one/two steps up and one/two steps sideways. I challenge you to pay attention to what you say, how you say, and who you say it too. We suit up for battle. We stand! The battle is not yours, it's the Lords. Arguing in the name of the gospel is not a good introduction to Christ. "The Lord put a word in my spirit," is often said. Was that word just for you or others?

On your purpose today are you listening to what you're supposed to say?

_____
_____
_____
_____

"Being abreast of what to say next should fall in line with whom it reaches. Speaking because of a self-edification pause is an ungodly cautionary procedure."

What's Your Label?

The world indulges in labels. People pick and choose what category to lock you into. Remembering the day you were baptized and filled with the Holy Ghost is fine. Refusing to count the day, year, and time Jesus delivered you from certain sins is freeing. Recollecting being 97lbs from smoking crack or my children being escorted from my custody does not help me. It's a testimony for those who need to know deliverance is possible. Announcing that I refused rehabilitation doesn't mean I shun the rehabilitation process, but to prove deliverance is possible when you sincerely ask God for it. It will be given unto you if you believe and receive it, and walk in faith. When I am asked, "How long has it been since you stopped using drugs?" I reply, "I don't know." (If I gave it some thought I could count the time, but, I don't). I respond that I simply walked in faith and was made whole. Jesus isn't counting, so why should I. Why are you?

Are there past labels that you or others try to hold over you?

_____
_____
_____
_____

He will turn again; he will have compassion upon us; he will subdue our iniquities; and thou wilt cast all their sins into the depths of the sea (Mic 7:19)

Being in the world, I understand your doubt. When asked when you last lied, fornicated, backstabbed, or walked in your own willful way, remember that deliverance is not particular. How can you put a restraint on omnipotence? Continuing to call yourself an addict/alcoholic because of past drug use or alcohol consumption is announcing that Jesus can only work in certain time segments or on certain things.

Please note that if you are going through something and think the only thing that you will get you through is a drink or drug; or if you can't deal with a situation and your mindset is a constant I will not use today, I will not use today; prayer and a meeting may be needed for you. When a problem arises and prayer is your first thought; faith is activated and victory is present. Jesus is a deliverer and a combatant for any drink or drug. Still calling yourself an addict, liar, thief, fornicator, adulterer, or alcoholic etc...is a trick of the enemy. You cannot be a delivered addict. Speak freedom and walk in it. If you ask, Jesus will forgive you of your sins and what man can come against you and deem you any different?

Hello, my name is _____ *and I have been delivered from*

_____
_____
_____
_____
_____
_____
_____
_____
_____
_____
_____
_____
_____
_____
_____
_____
_____
_____
_____
_____
_____
_____
_____
_____
_____
_____
_____
_____
_____

Are You In or Of?

Suspicious faith outlines the boundaries of this world. Contemplating the next move can be a set up for ritualizing your system. Anything out of the norm that you're relaxed in could cause a mental outburst, a spiritual breakdown, and a physical heartache. Trying to please this one to appease that one while keeping the other one calm is confusing even as I write it. "Out with the old and in with the new." What happens when the old becomes the new? You're frustrated because you've thrown the old away. You wake up to your repetitive morning routine. This shouldn't be if morning by morning new mercies you see. Why have hope in this world?

Admit it! What are you relaxed in?

_____
_____
_____
_____

And be not conformed to this world: but be ye transformed by the renewing of your mind, that ye may prove what is that good, and acceptable, and perfect, will of God (Rom 12:2)

Waking up with a praise on your lips amidst the aches in your body, the children arguing, that bad news phone call, and you haven't even left your room yet situations, can cease to move you in a negative way, but Jesus! A "not of this world mentality," opens your mindset. You are now aware of flesh and principalities. Holding on to anger makes no sense. Holding on to fear makes no sense. Holding on to someone or something that can only hinder an optimistic mood or thought just makes no sense. "Hate the sin and not the man it's in. Why? Because "We wrestle not against flesh and blood…," so pounce a prayer on it, "stamp a "in Jesus' name" on it, count it done, and walk by faith.

Recognizing being not of this world I…

_____
_____
_____
_____

In this world, the reason for nonsense is an attraction to man. Being not of this world, you know that nonsense is a distraction, its "principality's plan.

The Message In the Wilderness

Nobody is here. It's just you. Can you deal with you? This familiar or unfamiliar place is a time where you, your body, and Jesus convene. The reason I say your body and you is for the carnal man and the spiritual man. The spirit is willing to weather this wilderness. The weakness of the flesh is put on trial. The dictionary defines the wilderness as an inhospitable region. In other words it's not a great vacation. This is "man in the mirror" time. This is a process not a permanent dwelling. It's a test of control, sacrifice, submission, and faith. Can you override cravings of the flesh? Can you do without your wants? Can you give up a daily routine? Can you fully submit and do away with ritualistic practices? Is your faith secure in your wilderness endeavors?

In the wilderness my message was...

_____
_____
_____
_____

Then was Jesus led up of the Spirit into the wilderness to be tempted of the devil (Matt 4:1)

In this "New Testament" era we sincerely appreciate the grace and mercy bestowed upon us. Our faith, tempers, attitudes, thoughts, flesh, and verbal capabilities (and more) are tried in the fire on a daily basis. When that wilderness moment hits, it's time for all those earthly qualities to be subjected to His will. This wilderness time is strictly devoted to Jesus. During this particular time temptation is on a high. It can be stressful, but it's a two way street. While restoration is being implemented, the unnecessary is filtered out. This process is beneficial for your salvation. As Satan tried to tempt Jesus in the wilderness, I know that Jesus knew he had to get permission to do so. (What Satan offered Jesus was already His). Like he had to for Job, who lost all he had, is our mind settled in. "The Lord giveth and the Lord taketh away?" I came out of the wilderness with a new attitude!

_____
_____
_____
_____

There is growth in the wilderness!

Grateful Moments

This reflection of moments is to remind you of the grace, mercy, and favor in your life. Being humbled in appreciation can take the pride away and bridle some entitlement issues. His unconditional love is phenomenal. This flesh that surrounds our spirit can cloud our gratefulness. Being grateful puts you in the position of receiving. One of the words associated with grateful is thankful. One of the words associated with thankful is relieved. We aren't deserving of anything and His grace is sufficient. So, being grateful can relieve you from murmuring, complaining, being anxious, and having some unresolved regrets.

My grateful moments include…

_____
_____
_____
_____

In being grateful you realize His grace is sufficient. His mercy endures to all generations. Just the thought of Jesus' sacrifice on Calvary is awesome in itself. The blood that was shed in our stead is a cause to praise His name. Being able and allowed to say the name "Jesus" is a privilege. In other countries you can be killed upon sight calling on Jesus name. As we thank Him for giving us this day our daily bread ritually, I challenge you to speak gratefulness beyond the now.

Beyond this right now, I'm grateful for…

_____
_____
_____
_____

"Lord oh Lord I appreciate the blessing you bestowed upon me and the chastisement to position me for purpose."

Capacities

The word capacity is defined as being the maximum amount that something can contain. Studies state that we only use a portion of our brain. Teachers, professors, and instructors etc.. are always trying to urge us to widen our mindset. Tapping into broader territories of our brains or thought processes can shed new light on ways of doing things better or a different way to approach a problem or issue. There's always room for improvement. Financial status, education, or certain social positions may increase your capabilities, but does it always enlarge your capacity?

Are you spiritually living life in His fullness?

_____
_____
_____
_____

Behold I have set the land before you: go in and possess the land which the Lord swore unto your fathers, Abraham, Isaac, and Jacob, to give unto them and to their seed after them (Deut 1:8).

Your capacity can be enlarge as you mature in God. You wouldn't give a baby steak to eat. The child's body isn't ready. The teeth need to be present for chewing and the digestive system needs to be able to handle this upgrade of food. Being a newborn or not fully matured in Christ is not a bad thing. This process of growing in Christ prepares you for the blessings and trials that God has for us. In reading His word you will find that "the more you know the more you'll grow." He wants you to live beyond what your mind can conceive, but are you ready? The process of preparation will mold you to receive all He has for you.

Be anxious for nothing... (Phil 4:6)

Lord, in order to live internationally, I must...

_____
_____
_____
_____

"Open my eyes with understanding and let me see the point of change, change the point of changes."

Letting Go For Life

In order to receive what the Lord has for you, letting go the old things is very important. Relationships, social positions, bad habits, and other things that get in the way of your spiritual growth has to go. Everyone in your life can't go where God wants to take you. If you don't know what to let go of, or are in denial of what to let go of, prayer and hearing will let you know. Some of us wonder why our ministries have become stagnant or our growth seems to be in a pause. Changes need to be made by you! Holding on to the unnecessary can prolong the process. Even our thought process should change.

I will let go of... to move forward and upward.

_____
_____
_____
_____

To everything there is a season, and a time to every purpose under the heaven (Eccl 3:1)

Realizing that letting go of some people, places, and things can be trying. When you come to the fruition that in order for growth, you must let "Thy will be done," and surrender, the rewards are phenomenal and above anything that you could imagine. This leap of faith will cause mountains to crumble and burdens will be lifted. You didn't realize that because you were holding on to some people, places, and things, that it was keeping you from what God has for you. Those distractions can cause unnecessary irritability, stress, and confusion. I encourage you to "let go for life" more abundantly.

I realized that when I let go of.... I became more...

_____
_____
_____
_____

"Teach me oh Lord to bypass this mind of flesh in order to get to the spiritual core. I need to let go of the people, places, and things in order to receive the more in store for me."

Positioning For Purpose

The definitions for position and purpose are different, but when put together an awesome birth takes place. Positioning means to put or arrange someone or something in a particular way. Purpose means the reason why something is done or used. Example: You have a flower in your window. In order for it to fully bloom evenly you have to position it and reposition it. Jesus will position us and reposition us to fully flourish in purpose.

What position are you in right now?

_____
_____
_____
_____

And we know that all things work together for good to them that love God, to them who are the called according to his purpose (Romans 8:28)

God has a perfect plan. What has happened in our lives was known ahead of time. Every experience and encounter has been ordered by God. Some of them were very difficult. When reflecting on where God has brought you from, the here and now should override the back then. Are you aware of the times when you were positioned North to look up; East and West for instruction; and South, prostrate you for surrender? Our plans aren't perfect because our minds have boundaries and who knows what a tomorrow may bring. The word says "eyes have not seen nor ears heard…" (1 Cor 2:9). He has positioned our minds to ignore distractions and discern foolishness. He has positioned our emotions to know that being upset over what we can't control can interrupt and consume us. Since we cannot predict the future, moving in ordered steps with inclining ears, clears the spiritual path that redeems us for His purpose.

On purpose, when were you ordered to be still?

_____
_____
_____
_____

For thou hast possessed my reins: thou hast covered me in my mother's womb (Ps 139:13)

Complacency

The book of Jonah talks about how he refused to go where God sent him. During our life span some of us did not want to go or do what the Lord asked of us. We did the opposite or just refused. Yes, we have a choice! In pinball, once the ball springs into action, the goal is to get it to touch as many barriers, bells, tags, etc… to gain points. When it gets to where its about to go into the hole, two switches on the sides can project it back in action. We sometimes become comfortable in our mess and don't want to accept change or our lack of faith prevents us from change. Just as we become complacent, Jesus propels us back in action, sometimes by any means necessary.

I was comfortable in...

_____
_____
_____
_____

I went down to the bottoms of the mountains; the earth with her bars was about me forever: yet hast thou brought up my life from corruption, O Lord my God (Jonah 2:6)

When Jonah got on the ship to Tarshish, he wasn't aware that he put the people around him in danger. While the confusion and angry weather was going on, at the bottom of the ship lie Jonah asleep. *Jesus was peacefully asleep down in a ship while confusion and stormy weather was going on, but, Jonah wasn't. (Hmm, asleep while confusion was going on.)* Jonah told those on the boat who he, about his Lord whom he served, and how he refused to go where the Lord had sent him. He was ministering even in His mess. The men threw him off the boat. They also repented and made vows and acknowledged the true God. Jonah vividly explains how he was 'tossed to and fro.' He describes how the weeds were about his head and the water kept overtaking him. He was drowning in his mess. There are consequences for making bad decisions. This is where grace, mercy, and chastisement are at work. Jonah was spat out to do what God told him.

When I was put back in place I...

_____
_____
_____
_____

When the Lord calls, listening the first time is best or you'll repeat the same test

Continued Faith

My mother used to play an old record from a Gospel group, "The Caravans" called, "Where is Your faith in God?" The word, where, could suggest a location. Without knowing it, we put faith in our everyday living activities. Alarm clocks, stoves, cars, food, medicines, machinery, computers, advertisements, family members, the weather, co-workers, and other professionals have gained our trust. When those things break, shut down, don't perform properly, or people disappoint us, we get angry and frustrated, because our levels of expectations have been diminished. Yet, another day comes and we repeat those same practices. Trust and faith can be similar. Trust is defined as the strength, character, ability, or truth of something or someone in which we put confidence. Faith is defined as belief and trust.

Are you talking faith? Where and When is your Faith?

_____
_____
_____
_____

Now faith is the substance of things hoped for, the evidence of things not seen (Heb 11:1)

"And Jesus said unto them, Because of your unbelief: for verily I say unto you, If ye have faith as a grain of mustard seed, ye shall say unto this mountain, Remove hence to yonder place; and it shall remove; and nothing shall be impossible unto you" (Matt 17:20). The last part of this verse is rarely said or not included enough. "And nothing shall be impossible to you:" means continued, always, and as long as. Imagine the following;. Minor faith moving major things. Less of you and more of Him. Nothing into something. Inferior to superior. Decreased to be increased. Reduced to be induced. Mitigated to be vindicated. Watch the principalities eradicated in your life. By the way if your relationship in Jesus has years on it then your mustard seed faith should have increased by now. It says "*as* a mustard seed." What a mighty God we serve! I love Him!

Now faith, right this minute faith, abrupt faith… (add more and believe)

_____
_____
_____
_____

Faith overrides foolishness

Strongholds

Fornication, Deceit, Homosexuality, Low Self-esteem, Lying, Fear, Diseases Poverty, Long-suffering, Procrastination, Abuse of power, Pornography, Condemnation, Back–biting, Gossiping, Idol worship, Vindictiveness, Domestic violence, Lack of spiritual intelligence, Back-sliding, Lack of accountability, Hatred, Dishonest, Confusion and Turmoil, Complacency, Lack of Knowledge, Hunger, Wasted riches, Vain, Adultery, Hopelessness, Depression, Oppression, Recession, Sexual Abuse, Greed, Loneliness, Corruption in politics and governments. Bullying, False five-fold ministries, Palm readers, Tarot Card Readers, Sooth-Sayers and Psychics. False allegiances, Covetousness, Murdering, Predators and Perpetrators, Homelessness, Perversion, Lasciviousness, and Wars.

I's in the name of Jesus, we bind, and break-up these strongholds. We claim victory. Lord we ask that you restore, replenish, renew, and revive in us that which you have made us to be. In Jesus name replace the hatred in our hearts with love. Instill in us a clean heart and a stable mindset. Instill in us forgiveness in order for us to move on and live. We ask for forgiveness, and that you reduce us and incorporate you. Father we realize that we are beyond human help. The only thing that can bring us through is salvation. Lord take away the guilt and shame of our past so we may function in your kingdom successfully. Jesus as we diligently seek you please quiet the chaos and input the peace that was purposed in our lives. Jesus incline our ears, bridle our tongues, and keep our eyes on you in this world full of distractions. In Jesus name keep us in your word for our daily bread, every hour bread, every minute and every second bread. Saturate our lives with joy and love. Jesus we thank you for the victory because "…You so loved the world…" Jesus we thank you for a constant reminder that all things are possible in you. We will give your name the praise anyhow. We claim healing. We love and adore you Jesus. Amen!

For the weapons of our warfare are not carnal, but mighty through God to the pulling down of strong holds; (2 Cor 10:4)

*Write down some other strongholds. We have some personal ones. *(We think they're personal!)*

_____
_____
_____
_____

On Your Mark, Get Set, Stand!
QUESTIONS AND A CONCERNS

Have you ever felt bound, tied down, or weighed down? Have you ever contemplated a controversy which carried you through a crawl space trial? Where you can't, He can!

But now, O Lord, thou art our father; we are the clay, and thou our potter; and we all are the work of thy hand (Isa 64:8).

Has your mind been so heavy and fed up that you would start screaming right now if you didn't think that they'd lock you up right now! No one really sees the war going on inside you. They can't comprehend what it took to get you here, just now, right now, this very second! Cover me Jesus! Cover me Jesus! Cover me Jesus!

And the peace of God, which passeth all understanding, shall keep your hearts and minds through Christ Jesus (Phil 4:7)

How long Lord? How long? You're feeling as if this wilderness moment is going to take you out of here! You keep trusting! You've kept the faith! The 5 –Fold ministry has gotten involved. They've been standing in as proxy for you. It seems that Canaan Land won't be reached no time soon! I'm fasting and praying saying, "Yes Lord, I will be still."

Wait on the Lord, and keep his way, and he shall exalt thee to inherit the land: when the wicked are cut off, thou shalt see it (Ps 37:34)

I heard my daughter singing, "It's Time for a "Re-up." I'm discerning that your spiritual crisis calls for restoration and rejuvenation. You need to be redone, refilled renewed, and refueled, reestablished reclassified, and revitalized in order to be reached out to. Your spirit thirsts for, your spirit yearns for, and your spirit longs for that new creature in Christ Jesus.

But Jesus beheld them, and said unto them, With men this is impossible; but with God all things are possible (Matt 19:26)

Accept Him. It's just that easy. Ask for forgiveness and your yolk will be easy. Knock and the door shall be open unto you.

I indeed have baptized you with water: but he shall baptize you with the Holy Ghost (Mk 1:8)

The thief cometh not, but for to steal, and to kill, and to destroy: I am come that they might have life, and that they might have it more abundantly (Jn 10:10)

For the weapons of our warfare are not carnal, but mighty through God to the pulling down of strong holds (2 Cor 10:4)

When you understand that the fight isn't with man, it's with the principalities, try this weapon: **Obedience**!

On Your Mark, Get Set, Stand!

_____
_____
_____
_____
_____
_____
_____
_____
_____
_____
_____
_____
_____
_____
_____
_____
_____
_____
_____
_____
_____
_____
_____

Submit

We submit applications and forms. We submit, commit, compare, then regret. You click the submit button on the computer. If you did not complete or miss something, it reminds you of what is wrong or why you have failed, and sometimes there is a time limit. It's sometimes outlined in red. Starting over or repeating the steps or instructions can be mind boggling and/or tiresome. You become determined to get it right. Sometimes stop because of frustration. When I think of the word, "submit," it reminds me of words like; obey, consider, yield to, or surrender to, etc… Pride can stop you from submitting. Mistrust and authority issues can get in the way.

Whom do you submit to and is it in line with the word?

_____
_____
_____
_____

For they being ignorant of God's righteousness, and going about to establish their own righteousness, have not submitted themselves unto the righteousness of God" (Rom 10:3)

We realize that egos, personalities, Ethnicity, creed, sexuality... can be stumbling blocks when it gets down to the word "submit." Jesus gives us choices and boundaries while we still live in freedom. If you submit, there are things you have to resist. Pleasing Jesus should always be first and foremost. Submission comes with obedience. Obedience comes with discipline., Discipline comes with sacrifice. Sacrifice comes with salvation. Doing one without the other takes away from the former. When you aren't submitting to Christ you are committing wrong doings, and you aren't lined up with his will.

When I submit to the will of God I let go of

_____
_____
_____
_____

All of those lines were a distraction. The answer should have been "ME." Submit and become legit in the word of God.

Affordable Comfort

"Living above your means" is not a strange or unheard of truth. Man makes things seem so wonderful; and the subliminal messages have you thinking that you can afford just about anything. The credit cards enslave some of us to bankruptcy; or we find ourselves just cutting them up. Then something else comes along. Wants and needs keep the world's economy repetitious. Can we really afford the comforts in this world when it comes to salvation? I say no to some things, really a lot of things, which can distract or deter me in my walk with Jesus. What we did before salvation should be left with, what we did before salvation, because of a higher priority. Jesus paid a price that none of us could pay. Can you afford to be comfortable when ministry is 24/7? This comfort I'm talking about is not in the same class as a mansion, millions, that so called perfect job, entrepreneurship, Bentley etc…! I'm talking about an idle mind, casual spirit, ritualized relations and servicing churches opposed to church services.

Can you afford to tithe time to Jesus in you busy schedule?

_____
_____
_____
_____

Be sober, be vigilant; because your adversary the devil, as a roaring lion, walketh about, seeking whom he may devour: (I Pet 5:8)

And the Lord said, Simon, Simon, behold, Satan hath desired to have you, that he may sift you as wheat: (Lk 22:31)

The word says that we should not be slothful and lackadaisical. It specifies that if we keep our minds stayed on Jesus, peace will be provided. Yes, we make mistakes and yes, He will forgive and chastise us. There's freedom in comfort. He died for us and our sins can be washed away. He made comfort affordable and knowing that you are redeemed is a "Heavenly" comfort that is yours!

How are you comfortable in Jesus?

_____
_____
_____
_____

We can't possibly achieve the sacrifice that Jesus made. We can't perceive all that He has in store for us. Receive Him as your Savior. Believe that you are an overcomer. Live in purpose.

Parental Rights

Parental rights can be a touchy subject when it comes to discipline. This is due to the abuse and death that some parents have caused their children. Condemning your child is not the correct way. Condemnation brings on insecurity, self-esteem issues, and hopelessness. There are other ways to convince and teach your child. Being a good example doesn't always make your children good examples. Fussing, complaining, and threatening isn't doing any good either. For example, I was told the stove was hot, but I couldn't grasp that reality; and didn't believe it until I touched it. Some say that, "experience is the best teacher." What if you don't survive the experience? You are held accountable if someone told you about the consequences and you refused to listen. Talking until you're blue in the face can bring on frustration, anger, and separation. They go on about their business and you're at your wits end. Prayer works; maybe not as fast as you want it, but since your time and Jesus time is different it's on time. Raising children can be trying and rewarding.

As a parent I realize...

_____
_____
_____
_____

Furthermore we have had fathers of our flesh which corrected us, and we gave them reverence: shall we not much rather be in subjection unto the Father of spirits, and live (Heb 12:9)

Our Father (Jesus) does not condemn us for our sins or actions. Chastisement is His way. The enemy wants us to feel condemned, but Jesus forgives wholly. Being filled with the Holy Spirit will convict you of things that aren't pleasing to the Father. Presenting your body as a living sacrifice compels you to want to please the Father. Don't get it twisted, in the end damnation will remain for those who reject Him. Condemnation brings on fear and "God hasn't given us the spirit of fear..." As He teaches and molds us to His will, and for His purpose, mistakes will be made and corrections will be implemented with love. We are His children and that is the way of the Father.

As for me and my household we will...

_____
_____
_____
_____

For whom the Lord loveth he chasteneth, and scourgeth every son whom he receiveth. If ye endure chastening, God dealeth with you as with sons; for what son is he whom the father chasteneth not (Heb 12:6-7)

Spiritual Boomerang

The word boomerang has two meanings. One meaning describes it as a flat piece of wood that you can throw out and it will return to you. The other meaning speaks more of plans and/or actions being returned by the planner. When you say good morning, good afternoon or good evening, with a sincere heart in spite of what you're going through, You expect to get it back. Some may respond pleasantly. Some may respond robotically (which means you say it and they respond without thinking). Others may not even respond. If you're saying it in all sincerity, whatever the response is, your heart should be clear. As Christians being kind should always be your first thought.

When greeting or speaking to someone are you easily agitated when being cordial is not reciprocated?

_____
_____
_____
_____

Be not deceived; God is not mocked: for whatsoever a man soweth, that shall he also reap (Gal 6:7)

The word speaks about what you give out you shall receive and reaping and sowing. If your attitude or disposition is not Godly what kind of witness are you? What example can the lost see if God's own have temperaments of the world? What you sow you shall reap? Sowing discord amongst your brothers and sisters will come back to you. The world doesn't understand what the word is saying to them. Since you are among them, are you constantly gossiping and in agreement with them? They lash out against His own when they're not walking in His will. Are you living and being the exception to the rule and holding your tongue and suggesting prayer? Negativity thrown out brings negativity back. I'm glad that God doesn't give us our "just desserts." Grace and mercy is a wonderful thing.

Is what you are throwing out there something you want to receive?

_____
_____
_____
_____

If you sow the word, you will reap and receive the word!

A You're Excused Moment

The word "excused" is used many ways: an apology, pardon, forgive, free etc...In salvations plan it means that the blood of lambs, doves, and calves is no longer necessary or accepted. Jesus died for our sins and his sacrifice is now in place. Now if you're born again you're excused from all sin. No condemnation and no fear. Yes, all sin. This topic doesn't need much. If you can remember, and would like to go down memory lane, name some things that you are excused from.

No Substitutions

There is substitute sugar, crabmeat, cheese, teachers and so on. There is none other like Jesus. You can search the universe. You can try all the nouns: persons, places, or things. Jesus doesn't want substitutions. He will not take part of you, part time you, holiday you, or when you get in trouble you. Yes, he can save you from anything. He is not a "whenever you feel you need him, God. No, his grace and mercy isn't a product. He has no shelf life because, He is eternal. Yes, there is an expiration date for grace and mercy. Yes, He is omnipresent. Yes, the word "Daddy" can be over used. Jesus is not PRN (as needed). Don't confuse His resources when you just need a carnal rescue.

I tried to substitute Jesus when...

_____
_____
_____
_____

For false christs and false prophets shall rise, and shall shew signs and wonders, to seduce, if it were possible, even the elect (Mk 13:22)

In the old Testament there were animal sacrifices. Sacrificing an animal for blood served as redemption for sins committed. Those sacrifices had become void when Jesus died on the cross. Shedding blood is now obsolete. Let's consider the first sacrifice when Jesus clothed Adam and Eve in animal skins. Adam and Eve had disobeyed God and they saw themselves naked physically. God felt them naked and was disconnected from them. Wrong cannot dwell in Him! No matter what the critics, heretics, and atheist say, Jesus is real! Those who are calling themselves a god, a proxy, the master etc... cannot possess the power of the Almighty. Watch out for substitutes and embrace the real. His sheep hear his voice.

Who is like the Lord? (CIRCLE ONE PLEASE)

Man   **Creature**   **Thing**   **None**

The result of my Substitution is...

_____
_____
_____
_____

Be honest! You can't fool God!

The Herd Hears

A mother can hear her child's voice or cry in the midst of a crowd. The deaf are taught to feel rhythms. An animal can tell where their young are by smell, sound, or touch. Children are taught to follow certain family rules and standards. In the animal kingdom sometimes the young wonder off or are not close to the herd, pack or, clan. This can be very dangerous. Predators are always watching and waiting to kill and feast on the young and the weak.. It has been said that the pack is only as strong as the weakest one. If the immature aren't listening, they may miss the window of opportunity especially if the pack or herd is constantly moving.

Are you consistently listening and following the shepherd and not the flock who can sometimes be wolves in sheep's clothing?

_____

_____

_____

I am the good shepherd, and know my sheep, and am known of mine. As the Father knoweth me, even so know I the Father: and I lay down my life for the sheep. And other sheep I have, which are not of this fold: them also I must bring, and they shall hear my voice; and there shall be one fold, and one shepherd (Jn 10:14-16)

Are you aware of the shepherd's voice? I have heard people say the Father called them home. While in sin He calls you home. Backslider, come home. A herd does not travel in single file. They travel as a group looking out for each other. The stronger on the outside for protection until the immature grows and learned how to travel as a herd or group. This is the same for ministry. The older and stronger teach the weak and immature the importance of following the shepherd. The young are watching the strong. As the shepherd leads, if any strays, he goes and finds them. He carries them home, calling out so they can follow the sound of his voice. The herd trusts and obeys the shepherd.

Are your ears inclined to hear the shepherd or are you still following other sheep who have turned out to be wolves and have misled you?

_____

_____

_____

_____

Whether bumped or bruised the Shepherd calls. Allow his voice to lead your heart and soul.

Laboring The Birth

Man has invented all types of gadgets to mimic the pains that women feel while pregnant and giving birth. They've even invented an actual uterus to wear. So, instead of making this seem one-sided, let's talk spiritually. As your purpose and ministry comes forth there are some procedures for you. After realizing that you are purposed, tests are put in place. It has to be established that you can handle things. Can you deal with what comes with your ministry? How long is it going to take to birth this? Will it come on your terms? A C-section (C means Christ) is the best way spiritually. Your way won't even be acknowledge by God! The Father has this. Keep nourishing and feeding this ministry with the word, fasting, and praying. While doing these things Jesus is molding, forming, and shaping it. He's making a way. During this trial you may start to feel overloaded and bloated. This experience will make all that you've gone through worth it.

When You started your ministry how long were your labor pangs? Some of us are still laboring. It's okay cause it's all gain.

_____
_____
_____
_____

And the angel said unto her, Fear not, Mary: for thou hast found favour with God (Lk 1:30)

Can you imagine being Mary's when the angels said to her thou hast found favor with God? Your ministry and purpose is about to come forth. The growth proceeds and your soul rises to the occasion. This process is about to birth and be shared throughout the world. Why settle for local when international is possible? People have been in ministry for decades and wonder why someone who started one year ago has passed where they are, currently. Favor ain't fair! An effective ministry is not a waste of time. Some long-timers have become ritualized in their relationship with Jesus and new wine in an old container serves no purpose.

_____
_____
_____
_____

What has God birthed in you?

Contact

When you say contact, you think of a connection. When your soul makes that Holy connection, it's awesome. Longevity in Jesus is beautiful. That zeal for a relationship in Jesus during that first contact is breath taking. If it isn't fed continuously, that feeling and hunger will become mediocre. How can we as Christians allow new people in Christ to become malnourished in their walk in Jesus? Heaven rejoices when someone is saved and so should we. In blessing the Lord at all times we should never be slack in His service. We should encourage babes in Christ to want more in their relationship. They should not have to suffer rules and regulatory strategies that can set them back. Jesus strengthens the kingdom. Judgment is not our business. Saving someone is out of our hands. Jesus saves! Our living should be a witness and not just our conversation.

Can you describe your first contact with Jesus? Now, is "every day with Jesus is sweeter than the day before?"

_____
_____
_____
_____

Wherefore comfort yourselves together, and edify one another, even as also ye do (1 Thess 5:11)

As we edify one another the glory of Jesus should be the premise of our praise. Can we ever afford to be slack in Jesus? No, because morning by morning new mercies we see. Jesus has already paid the ultimate price. It had to be him. Neither James, Peter, nor John could fulfill this position, because of the corruptible seed in man. So a thief, prostitute, backslider, adulterer, murderer etc… never paid for redemption because Jesus paid it all. So remember, during that contact and connect with a meaning.

When you walk away after having a conversation with someone what's on their mind? Have you left the person with a thought of Jesus, kingdom building, love thy neighbor, having a better relationship with Christ, or a What can I do to be saved mindset?

_____
_____
_____
_____

Make sure your claim to walk with Jesus is evident in your contacts!

Acceptable Rejects

Throughout history, people have been rejected because of skin color, sex, origin, creed, disabilities, and beliefs. This is usually because of fear, ignorance, hatred, and/or following the crowd. In this age, the same reasons are in play. People learn to hate behind doors, products, conversations, and abilities. When going on a job interview, you are usually submit a resume that introduces who you are and what you have done. When you leave the interview, personnel either accepts or rejects you. Sometimes it's face to face, phone call, letter, email or just no response. While waiting, we can become worried, anxious, and agitated. We can also feel rejected in families and in relationships. Our bank card or credit card can be rejected for insufficient funds. Either way, the feeling isn't pleasant. You can wallow in it or pretend it didn't happen. Addressing the person is not a good idea, unless you're instructed by God. Otherwise move on!

When have you felt rejected?

_____
_____
_____
_____

And have ye not read this scripture; The stone which the builders rejected become the head of the corner (Mk 12:10)

This feeling can be taken lightly if you have that "of the world mentality." Jesus was rejected because of a supreme plan. We say we wouldn't have rejected Him, but the plan had to be fulfilled. These days, rejecting Him is common place. In some countries, you can be killed for saying His name. I thank Jesus that in this country freedom of religion is still in place. The Apostolic doctrine is my way of living. The world will reject you, but Jesus won't! Jesus' ultimate sacrifice established redemption. Thank you Jesus!

Knowing that even Jesus was rejected I look at things differently because...

_____
_____
_____
_____

The stone that the builders rejected was a sacrifice for man. It had to be, because of Salvation's plan.

Necessary Demonstrations

When you go to malls and grocery stores there are always demonstrations to prove a product or foods status, goodness, abilities, and capabilities. They would like you to purchase, buy in, or lay-a-way something. At home, your parents are always proving that they love you. They instill abilities for a positive outcome for society. Teachers teach, preachers preach, and your peers advise.

What demonstration/s made an impact in your life?

_____
_____
_____
_____

And, behold, there was a great earthquake: for the angel of the Lord descended from heaven, and came and rolled back the stone from the door, and sat upon it (Matt 28:2)

Some Biblical demonstrations were just for us. These proved who God is and all of His awesomeness: Read or reread the scriptures!

- ☐ Parables: Prodigal Son, The Vineyard, The Wise and Foolish Man, The Rich Man and the Poor man (Matt 13:13)
- ☐ The Parting of the Red Sea (Ex 14)
- ☐ David and Goliath (1 Sam 17)
- ☐ Samson (Judg 16)
- ☐ The Woman with the Issue of Blood (Mk 5)
- ☐ Feeding the 5,000 (Matt 14)
- ☐ Ezekiel and the Bones (Ezek 37)
- ☐ Job (Job)
- ☐ Abraham (Gen 22)
- ☐ Woman at the Well (John 4)
- ☐ The Wall Of Jericho (Heb 11)

What can you add to this List?

_____
_____
_____
_____

Every demonstration is a notification!

It's In The Presentation

Did someone ever ask you to try something or invest your money in something and it did not look appealing? Some foods won't ever look appealing. If you have ever been house hunting, then you have some sense of the word "presentation." The outside is appealing and pleasant, but when you walk through the inside, it looks chaotic. Colors are clashing, paint is cleverly concealing water damages, the fireplace is clogged, and the steps are not only squeaky but they're uneven. Restaurants and fast food places can turn you off because of the attitudes of the waiters, cashiers etc… If the frontline isn't pleasant, then it really doesn't matter whether the food is good or bad. You'll leave and spend your hard earn money somewhere else.

Remember the time when a place's presentation did not meet your standards?

_____
_____
_____
_____

"I beseech you therefore, brethren, by the mercies of God, that ye present your bodies a living sacrifice, holy, acceptable unto God, which is your reasonable service." (Rom 12:1)

Your body is presentation may be big, little, light, dark, smart, not so smart, young or old. Jesus sees past our carnal ways after receiving Him. The inside overwhelms the outside. Your presentation to Him is a reflection of Him. Without him your dirt is dirt and life does not reside in you. When he resides the living waters will wash you a new look. Yes, the blood of the lamb will keep you, sustain you in life, preserve you, and that frame, is your reasonable service.

What physical, mental, and spiritual changes did you receive when saved?

_____
_____
_____
_____

If there was no change, we are praying for you! Amen!

The Well In The Desert

The state of being thirsty means to really want or need liquid. The younger generation uses it as a slang for the word desperate. It's not a good feeling being parched, dry, cracked, arid, or barren. Can you imagine being in such a dry place spiritually that you've surpassed human help? There aren't many nourishing places or things in your desert. Can you imagine that there is so much rain in the desert that it floods? People are walking around thirsting for love, hope, compassion, and change etc... I read of a certain woman who was not aware that she was in need of a living well in her parched life. (Jn 4)

Can you describe a hallelujah moment in your life when you experienced a spiritual quenching?

_____
_____
_____
_____

Jesus answered and said unto her, If thou knewest the gift of God, and who it is that saith to thee, Give me to drink; thou wouldest have asked of him, and he would have given thee living water (Jn 4:10)

Jesus was unknown to this Woman of Samaria. He's the Son of God, the well that shall never run dry, in human form. After reading this story you will know that her life was in a dry state. The first magnificent part is He came down to Samaria to see her. He came to her location. He meets us too! Upon sight she recognized him as a Jew which says she had a carnal eye for looks, but spiritually she was blind. After questioning her, and she questioning Him, both of them received the correct answers. She called Him a prophet and said that her people were waiting for the Messiah. When the disciples caught up to Him, He then provided them with spiritual meat. He did not only quench the thirst for this woman, but also spiritually fed the disciples whom at this time needed to be told more about his assignment. That my readers was a spiritual meal that the whole town and the disciples feasted upon.

What else do you get from this story?

_____
_____
_____
_____

Greetings

Have you ever entered in someone's home or place of business and before you got inside your destination, you were greeted unpleasantly. There have been times when I went to the house of the Lord and was greeted in an unkind manner. Coming from the outside to a place where peace, praise, and tranquility should abide, and instead be greeted with words of unpleasantness is rough and ungodly. You must look a certain way, you must smell a certain way, don't sit there, or sit back here. Having a stranger visit, belittle them, and tell them that they're not fit for your place of worship is horrible. At times when altar call is made that middle isle can be intimidating. I've even been asked to stop speaking when I was asked at the altar, "what ails you child of God", because of my illness or condition. Feeling condemned in God's house is wrong.

How do you think anyone should be greeted at the sanctuary door?

___
___
___
___

I was glad when they said unto me, Let us go into the house of the Lord (Ps 122:1).

Good tidings and cheer is an awesome greeting when you say it from the heart. "Praise the Lord," should always be as an instruction. It's not just correct in grammar, but it should also be followed by a praise report or hallelujahs. We have been so well tuned to just say "praise the Lord" back that it takes from the entire salutation. Most times it's answered back without a thought.

Let's practice: "Praise the Lord"

___
___
___
___
___
___
___
___

My Comings and Goings

The parable of the "Prodigal Son" (Lk 15:11), addresses coming back to the fold after realizing that this world is not friendly and has nothing to offer. If you think you need to test that water, please take my advice. Know that in Jesus there is no confusion nor calamity. Without Him you will fall to despair. So the son left and came back. During the life of Noah the rains came and left. In this segment we realize that Jesus always does two things. If Jesus is taking, He's giving. Or if He's giving, He's taking. Coming back to Jesus doesn't require much. Some people think that they have to be perfect before coming to Jesus. The father ran out to greet the prodigal son because of his willingness to come back. Some others feel too condemned to come back. Condemnation is not his way. It's the trick of the enemy to keep you wallowing in the mud with the pigs.

Come back to Jesus. He's waiting. What's your excuse?

_____
_____
_____
_____

That excuse is not worth your life. Come back He's waiting. All you have to do is ask!

Read the story again and get more from it. Every time I read this Jesus reveals something new.

What else did you get from this Parable?

_____
_____
_____
_____
_____
_____
_____
_____
_____
_____
_____
_____

Case Dismissed

Have you ever been accused of something that you didn't do? Really, who hasn't? (If you haven't, live longer.) It makes you feel strange. Some have been accused of so much, that it has been spoken over their lives. Some parents say to their child you're just like… (the absent/present parent). If you have ever been to court or a trial, they ask you, "What do you plead?" Are you guilty or not guilty? Imagine the prosecutor naming all of your past sins; and the jury sighing with ooos and aahs. After reading the list, for some of us a long one, and just as the list overwhelms even you, the judge bangs the gavel saying case dismissed. That is a hallelujah moment, a praise report, and a go ahead and shout victory dance! Jesus has done so much for us.

Can you write down a praise report or a hallelujah moment?

_____
_____
_____
_____

For all have sinned, and come short of the glory of God (Romans 3:23)

One day Jesus died on the cross for all of us. The "Sacrificial Lamb" has come to give his life to repair the communicative line that was broken in the Garden of Eden. The repairer of the breach, the stone that the builders rejected, the I Am that I Am, the mighty Rose of Sharon says, "cased dismissed saved by grace."

And they that shall be of thee shall build the old waste places: thou shalt raise up the foundations of many generations; and thou shalt be called, The repairer of the breach, the restorer of paths to dwell in (Isa 58:12)

For by grace are ye saved through faith; and that not of yourselves: it is the gift of God: Not of works, lest any man should boast (Eph 2:8-9)

What are some of your cases that have been dismissed? Feel free to shout!

_____
_____
_____
_____

CASE DISMISSED!

The Skin We're In

Incased in this image is a soul, spirit, and heart. Our outside has many names: dermis, epidermis, shell, crust, house, outer-layer, cast, and veil etc... How you treat your outside doesn't always agree with the inside. Your mind suggested piercings, make-up, tattoos, jewelry, clothes, perfumes, bruises, cuts, etc... Your skin did not request it. Sometimes we have regrets for what we have done to our skin. Pain is subjected to the mind. Whether it's intentional or not. When the veil was torn grace and salvation came forth. Just as Adam and Eve's sin was revealed in the Garden of Eden God used skin to cover them. The first animal sacrifice to cover us. Our outside, at times, doesn't represent the inside as the two should be on one accord. WE should be spiritually giving and physically letting go. Jesus underwent a lot of pain on the outside; the inside had achieved its goal. Being on one accord doesn't mean we have to look alike! Children of God should sound alike! What sound are you making?

Can you write down some things you put your skin through and how the inside kept the outside?

_____
_____
_____
_____

Your soul thirsts and hungers for righteousness so, how do you get the inside to reconstruct your outside. You don't, others will try, but Jesus provides the way as He is the way the Truth and the Life (Jn 14:6). As we age, Jesus is a keeper. The inside starts taking residence on the outside and he is Glorified. He can turn your anger into kindness and your hatred to love.

Write down some changes that he's done on the inside to make the outside invisible.

_____
_____
_____
_____

Hate the sin and not the skin it's in!
Lord mold us to you for your Glory!

No Returns and No Refunds

When I was delivered from crack-cocaine I never looked back. Hallelujah! Thank you Jesus! He is a keeper. The church mothers used to sing, "Somebody Prayed For Me. They had me on their mind." Prayer saved my life. I was down to 97 pounds and on my way out. I'm grateful Jesus Him spared my life. I would be selfish to think He spared it just for little old me. My testimony frees me, as it will free whom the Lord says. I have been restored to the purpose meant for me. Whoever this testimony frees, know it's like a chain reaction. As you speak freedom, it goes to another and another building the kingdom for His glory. In Jesus name, only free people can free people!

Name something that you did not return to when you were delivered from it!

_____
_____
_____
_____

So shall my word be that goeth forth out of my mouth: it shall not return unto me void, but it shall accomplish that which I please, and it shall prosper in the thing whereto I sent it (Isa 55:11)

Did you ever yell across a terrain, hallow room, or canyon? Whatever you said, the last part made a significant echo. It was the last word, but after a couple of times it faded away. Well God's word will never fade or return to Him void. It will accomplish what was said. It will fix, find, figure out, free, and bear fruit. Because you did not hear it doesn't mean it won't do what was said. Abraham, (Gen 18:20) tried to change God's mind; but just prolonged the inevitable and Lots wife was killed for trying to look back. The incident concerning a fig tree is very powerful. (Matt 21:19) Jesus waved his hand to it and never looked back. To this day no one has returned to the Garden of Eden. The price Jesus paid for our sins is non-refundable. His work is finished. He sits on the right hand of the Father.

What is your purpose?

_____
_____
_____
_____

"Though your purpose came through you, it's not for you. It's for another to endure the walk."

Expectable

Suitable you. A lot of us are people pleasers. You will wear yourself out. People change like the weather. Some just please themselves on a selfish status. Those who are concerned about their soul, please God. Not to say we don't fall short, but our aim is to please Him. When in a relationship with Jesus you understand what he expects from you. "But he that knew not, and did commit things worthy of stripes, shall be beaten with few stripes. For unto whomsoever much is given, of him shall be much required: and to whom men have committed much, of him they will ask the more" (Lk 12:48). It's a different look for all, but the worship and praise should be on one accord. Day by day new mercies are handed down to suitable you. The air you breathe, the nature you see, your support system , family and friends, and your body are mercies from God. Jesus goes out His way for His sheep as they are fed on His word and incline their senses to the shepherd. Yes, the herd has strays, sick, and some are overzealous. Yes, the herd can be faithful, prayerful, and gifted and talented, but that is His flock.

Who are you in Jesus' flock?

_____
_____
_____
_____

Who shall change our vile body, that it may be fashioned like unto his glorious body, according to the working whereby he is able even to subdue all things unto himself (Phil 3:21)

All have a purpose and whatever you are going through doesn't change your assignment. Thank you Jesus! He refines us and molds us for specific uses suitable to your soul. Moses served his season, Abraham served his season, Jonah, certain Kings, and the disciples served their season. Their seeds have helped to refine the access given us by God. Stand proud, and stand firm. As we are conformed for God's will. Being in the world you don't recognize Jesus and your focus is just to suit you.

What does Jesus tell you to change?

_____
_____
_____
_____

Change your ways for better days.

And Then There Were None

In the book of Revelations John wrote to the seven churches. He mentions over and over "He that hath an ear let him hear what the spirit saith unto the churches" (Rev 2:29). This suggests that you to listen up.

In the letter to **Ephesus** he spoke about restoration. Deliverance is free. Say yes to His will. Come back because you left Him. He did not leave you. "...I will never leave thee, nor forsake thee"(Heb' 13:5).

He wrote to **Smyrna** concerning perseverance. Hang in there. Jesus died on a Friday and arose on Sunday. Don't faint! "Tho He slay me yet will I trust Him" (Job 13:15). Stay with me cause "Sunday is coming."

Concerning **Pergamos** he asked them to watch out for false doctrines. You've got to know that you know that you know. Stay in His word. "My people are destroyed for lack of knowledge:" (Hos 4:6). Don't try to relax the word to suit your carnal man.

Thyatira needed to realize that the veil was torn. Confessions to a priest was no longer necessary. Just look up or to the side. He has no boundaries. So have a little talk with Jesus and tell him all your troubles. Whenever! And, behold, the veil of the temple was rent in twain from the top to the bottom; and the earth did quake, and the rocks rent" (Matt 27:51).

When he wrote to **Laodicea** he asked them to, basically, pick a side. Either you are up or down, or in or out. "For it had been better for them not to have known the way of righteousness, than, after they have known it, to turn from the holy commandment delivered unto them" (2 Pet 2:21).

He wanted to know "what" and "who" the church of **Sardis** works represented. "God is a Spirit: and they that worship him must worship him in spirit and in truth" (Jn 4:24).

Philadelphia **A**sk, **S**eek **K**nock. In your carnal eye in the streets you see pimps, thieves, drug addicts, and prostitutes. Jesus sees pastors, prophets, evangelist, and apostles.

Finally, my Brethren, I say that:

The church is in you **Ephesus** you can be restored.

The church is in you **Smyrna** persevere through persecution.
The church is in you **Pergamos** don't tolerate false doctrines. Keep and stay in the word. Heed the voice of the shepherd and don't follow the crowd.
The church is in you **Thyatira** realize that you are under a new covenant.
The church is in you **Laodicea** follow Jesus and not seducing spirits. Straddling the fence is not a choice. Get your mind together.
The church is in you **Sardis** Are you living like the Pharisees and Sadducees because God sees and turns away. Worship the Lord in truth and in spirit. There is nothing worse than a spiritual misfit.
The church is in you **Philadelphia** Don't let what is here on earth keep you here on earth.

Which church have you been delivered from?

_____
_____
_____
_____

I'm trying my best not to be left here. So I'm focused on Heaven.

Moments of Sunshine And Rainy Days

Any day above ground is a good day. Rainy days are nice. When the sun is shining and its about 80° some of us describe that as a perfect day. Realizing what the sun does and what the rains does makes you appreciate both. As the sun shines certain nutrients are obtained from it. Certain insects come out and pollenate the plants as they go from plant to plant. Some seeds are carried or blown to create more plants. Let's be clear, "mother nature" is not at work. Jesus has his hands on everything since the "earth is the Lord's" (Ps 24:1). The rain also plays a part in growth. Yes, those rainy days serve a purpose. For most plants rain is the most precious part of their world. The sun can burn and dry up just as the water can flood the lands. The word moment suggests a short time. We know that a day consists of 24 hours, but since we are on God's time, who knows what a moment is?

What exists in your sunny days and rainy days?
_____
_____
_____

"And they waited for me as for the rain; and they opened their mouth wide as for the latter rain" (Job 29:23).

Open your mouth and receive what the Lord has promise! Let Him get a grip of your carnal man and subdue it to the spirit. Man has a thirst for foolishness. This arid feeling can only be quenched by living water. Living water flows consistently. Stagnant water holds no life. Too much sun and you'll burn; too much water and you will drown. This is interesting because, both of them can complement each other. Let's talk about the latter rain. Scientist have said that the first rain cleans the air from impurities and heaviness. The second rain is more pure when it hasn't rained for a while. This is the rain that shall spring up in your wilted spirit.. More thirst quenching blessings. When you experience dryness its time for more. It's time for the arid to become moist. The moisture from the latter rain is bringing the blessings of the overflow and spiritually growth. Bring the latter rain my spirit thirsts for.

Bring the latter rain so my soul may be quenched and comforted.
_____
_____
_____
_____

Open your mouth and praise the Lord.

The Message, The Messenger, and The Messiah

(Message) "But of the tree of the knowledge of good and evil, thou shalt not eat of it: for in the day that thou eatest thereof thou shalt surely die." (Gen 2:17). **(Messenger)** "And the serpent said unto the woman, Ye shall not surely die." (Gen 3:4). **(Messiah)** "And she shall bring forth a son, and thou shalt call his name Jesus: for he shall save his people from their sins. Now all this was done, that it might be fulfilled which was spoken of the Lord by the prophet, saying, Behold, a virgin shall be with child, and shall bring forth a son, and they shall call his name Emmanuel, which being interpreted is, God with us." (Matt 1:21-23).

(Message) "And the Lord said, I will destroy man whom I have created from the face of the earth." (Genesis 6:7) **(Messenger)** "And the dove came in to him in the evening; and, lo, in her mouth was an olive leaf pluckt off." (Gen 8:11). **(Messiah)** "And death and hell were cast into the lake of fire. This is the second death." (Rev 20:14).

(Message) "And God said, Sarah thy wife shall bear thee a son indeed; and thou shalt call his name Isaac: and I will establish my covenant with him for an everlasting covenant, and with his seed after him" (Genesis 17:19). **(Messenger)** "And the angel of the Lord called unto him out of heaven, and said, Abraham, Abraham: and he said, Here am I. And Abraham lifted up his eyes, and looked, and behold behind him a ram caught in a thicket by his horns: and Abraham went and took the ram, and offered him up for a burnt offering in the stead of his son" (Gen 22:11,13). **(Messiah)** "Behold, a virgin shall be with child, and shall bring forth a son, and they shall call his name Emmanuel, which being interpreted is, God with us" (Matt 1:23). "For God so loved the world, that he gave his only begotten Son, that whosoever believeth in him should not perish, but have everlasting life (John 3:16).

(Message) "Now a certain man was sick, named Lazarus, of Bethany, the town of Mary and her sister Martha. When Jesus heard that, he said, This sickness is not unto death, but for the glory of God, that the Son of God might be glorified thereby." (Jn 11:1,4). **(Messenger)** "Then said Martha unto Jesus, Lord, if thou hadst been here, my brother had not died." "Jesus saith unto her, Said I not unto thee, that, if thou wouldest believe, thou shouldest see the glory of God." (Jn 11:21,40) **(Messiah)** "And he that was dead came forth, bound hand and foot with graveclothes: and his face was bound about with a napkin. Jesus saith unto them, Loose him, and let him go." (Jn 11:44).

(Message) To what purpose is the multitude of your sacrifices unto me? saith the Lord: I am full of the burnt offerings of rams, and the fat of fed beasts; and I delight not in the blood of bullocks, or of lambs, or of goats." (Isa 1:11) "And to love him with all the heart, and with all the understanding, and with all the soul, and with all the strength, and to love his neighbour as himself, is more than all whole burnt offerings and sacrifices." (Mk 12:33). **(Messenger)** "When Pilate saw that he could prevail nothing, but that rather a tumult was made, he took water, and washed his hands before the multitude, saying, I am innocent of the blood of this just person: see ye to it." (Matt 27:24) "And, we indeed justly; for we receive the due reward of our deeds: but this man hath done nothing amiss" (Lk 23:41). **(Messiah)** "And about the ninth hour Jesus cried with a loud voice, saying, Eli, Eli, lama sabachthani? that is to say, My God, my God, why hast thou forsaken me." (Matt 27:46). "For I delivered unto you first of all that which I also received, how that Christ died for our sins according to the scriptures; "(1 Cor 15:3).

(Message) "And Jesus said unto him, Verily I say unto thee, Today shalt thou be with me in paradise." (Lk 23:43). **(Messenger)** "And when Jesus had cried with a loud voice, he said, Father, into thy hands I commend my spirit: and having said thus, he gave up the ghost" (Lk 23:46). **(Messiah)** "And Jesus said unto him, Verily I say unto thee, Today shalt thou be with me in paradise" (Rev 1:18). "And there appeared unto them cloven tongues like as of fire, and it sat upon each of them." (Acts 2:3).

What's In A home?

If Jesus knocked on your door would you be prepared to answer? Whether it's a mansion or efficiency, He will knock. Are you in the position to receive company? Upon entering, is everything appearing to be in place? When your company comes, are you sweeping mess under the rug as if they wouldn't see the lumps? Are the closets so full of junk that it puts pressure on the closet doors? These hiding places are full because of the lack of preparation on the homeowner. Well the house looks nice on the outside, but as you look closer you start seeing the cracks. During the storm, does the roof leak? Good thing that your company is Jesus a "Mr. Fix-it!" Hopefully it's not "Mr./ Ms. Tear it down!

What are some of the repairs made in your life? Some of us had to get the foundation rebuilt. That's okay because on other ground is sinking sand.

_____
_____
_____
_____

Therefore whosoever heareth these sayings of mine, and doeth them, I will liken him unto a wise man, which built his house upon a rock:" And the rain descended, and the floods came, and the winds blew, and beat upon that house; and it fell not: for it was founded upon a rock (Matt 7:24-25)

Preparation is key, Dust those seemingly white lies off the surfaces. Scrub those floors to see your path clearly. Those dirty walls were really barriers. Rearrange some things and put them in the correct order. Open the curtains for clearer vision. Are all the bulbs working to shed the correct lighting for any situation?

What kind of cleaning does your spiritual home need for order?

_____
_____
_____
_____

What's in a home? Remember the watchman watching in vain?

Except the Lord build the house, they labour in vain that build it: except the Lord keep the city, the watchman waketh but in vain (Ps 127:1)

The Light In The Lighthouse

The only thing that matters is the brightness of the light. The house serves no purpose if there is nothing in it. Did you get that message? During the day you can clearly see the structure. When the night in your life presents itself, not only does the light shine in one direction, it illuminates the whole area and does extra by spinning around. You might not even see the infrastructure, but you are aware that it's there and even the rocks and waves have succumb to the brightness of the light. Halleluiah!

He illuminated the dark parts when...

_____
_____
_____
_____

Then spake Jesus again unto them, saying, I am the light of the world: he that followeth me shall not walk in darkness, but shall have the light of life (Jn 8:12)

Jesus in all his glory outshines anything. The waves and rocks that you see from afar don't even matter because, you know not to approach that shallow area. Those cliffs and jagged rocks are clearly seen when the light bares on it and also spiritually. The keeper has to make sure the light is kept. As time goes by the light adorns the lighthouse. It is upgraded to meet the storms as they might get unbearable. The light's direction is to hover over the whole area.

Does your light need adjusting? In all ministries, growth is supposed to happen.

_____
_____
_____
_____

Hide it under a bush? No! I will let it shine!

_____
_____
_____
_____
_____

The Fork In The Road

The devil doesn't want you to have it; and he doesn't want you to succeed. He doesn't want you to know that "what God has for you is for you." He knows that God has a plan for you. He knows that you're heaven bound. He knows he knows that the tests and trials you go through won't always be around. Satan doesn't want to hear your prayers and hear you say "in the name of Jesus." He doesn't want you to recall the sacrifice Jesus made for us. Satan wants you to live far beneath your means.

He knows that you're a child of God and he knows what that means. He loves the idle bickering, distractions and confusion. He is against the will of God and this is not an Illusion. He's aware that you can have that car, that home and peace of mind. He does not want you to get that job, have a spouse, a relationship with Jesus and love. His plan is to keep you blind. Don't lean to your own understanding at the fork in the road. Heed the voice of the savior. Be baptized and filled with the Holy Ghost. Hold on solider in the army of the Lord. Lean on Jesus for that eternal reward. Declare that the earth is the Lord's and all praises belong to God. He gets the glory and you have been absolved.

"Be sober, be vigilant; because your adversary the devil, as a roaring lion, walketh about, seeking whom he may devour (1Pet 5:8)

What happened when you came upon the "Fork In The Road?"

_____
_____
_____
_____

"The path isn't always clear but it's always present."

_____
_____
_____
_____
_____
_____
_____
_____
_____
_____

The Off Switch

A light switch can be turned off and on manually, by remote, by motions, or clapping. As Christians we don't always know when to stop, pause, or move. Jesus has instilled in us an off switch. The Holy Spirit will let you know, if consulted, when to move. The off switch is simply a be still moment. It doesn't always feel good but He knows best. Being in ministry is 24/7. Take time to minister to yourself and praise and worship the Lord. It has been said that, "until a door is open, praise him in the hallway."

When you tried moving and He said "be still," what happened?

_____
_____
_____
_____

Be still, and know that I am God: I will be exalted among the heathen, I will be exalted in the earth (Ps 46:10)

Going against his will has caused unauthorized allegiances, contending with wolves in sheep's clothing, illnesses, fence straddling, unnecessary offenses to the body, ill-gotten gain, and being bent to the will of others. This is a dangerous place. The only thing that will bring you back is His love, mercy, and grace. Thank you Jesus. It's time to fast and pray. Yes, he forgives. It's not always revealed why you should be still. Just trust Him.

_____
_____
_____
_____

The Master knows when to keep you from disasters. Father knows best!

_____
_____
_____
_____
_____
_____

Stakeholders

Many become five-fold leaders because of the mindset of, "what's in it for me?" They haven't been called by God. They are money hungry, power thirsty, and carnal minded seducers. This top dog mentality will trickle down all the way to the office receptionist. Everything is spiritually ineffective but motivationally captivating and stimulating to the carnal mind. Oh yes, the pockets of this damning, deceivable corporation and the entourage that precedes it is very dangerous to those who are not rooted or grounded correctly. They fall prey to anything. Instead of church meetings, they are holding corporate debriefings on the saints of God.

Shame on you.

"Beloved, believe not every spirit, but try the spirits whether they are of God: because many false prophets are gone out into the world" (1 Jn 4:1).

"But there were false prophets also among the people, even as there shall be false teachers among you, who privily shall bring in damnable heresies, even denying the Lord that bought them, and bring upon themselves swift destruction" (2 Pet 2:1).

Those in ministry along the side of you are praying for you until your ministry surpasses or becomes in their eyes bigger or more effective than theirs. It just might be, because scornful is really how they feel. Time wore down what they concealed. Plotting and planning against God's people in hallways and halfway closed doors. We see you!

Beware of false prophets, which come to you in sheep's clothing, but inwardly they are ravening wolves (Matt 7:15)

This is not a time for notes. (but there is some space below) It's a time for prayer. Asking the Lord to strengthen you and continue to nourish you in the word.

*Do you know who is on the Lord's side? Intercessory prayer, fasting, and discernment plays a good part in knowing that you know, that you know, that you know!

Be aware of your sidelines

_____
_____
_____
_____
_____

Essions/Distractions

THIS SECTION DEALS WITH WORDS THAT END IN "ESSION." SEARCH THE BIBLE FOR EXAMPLES OR ADD TO THEM.

AGGRESSION - To act in a forceful manner; assertive:
Pharaoh and Herod demonstrated aggression to the people over whom they ruled. They demonstrated aggression when it came to the birth of Moses and Jesus. Both came to free others. Moses helped free them physically and mentally. Jesus freed the Jews and Gentles spiritually. In this day bullies and people in authority at times might abuse their power whether someone is looking or not.

CONFESSION - Admission, declaration, revelation or, statement:
Adam confessed to eating the forbidden fruit. Cain confessed to killing Abel. The thieves on both sides of Jesus confessed that their punishment fit the crime. Some go to Priest to confess.

DIGRESSION - Detour, or to stray:
Jonah was supposed to go to Nineveh and went to Tarshish. Paul was on the road to Damascus for no good thing and was detoured to a house.

DEPRESSION - Sadness, misery, despair:
The Ten lepers were not happy with their situation; The woman with the issue of blood was sadden by her condition; The man at the pool had issues; Jeremiah was not his happiest because of the judgments from God for Jerusalem and Judah…

PROFESSION - Occupation, career, business, work:
Pharisees, and Sadducees were Judges (even though they were hypocrites). Solomon and David were great kings.

OPPRESSION - Harassment, cruelty, domination:
The Egyptian oppressed the Jews. The Colonist oppressed the Native Americans. The Germans oppressed the Jews. The British oppressed the Asians and Africans. Let all of this go and move forward in Christ!

Are you paying too much attention to any of these distractions

_____
_____
_____

Focus on Heaven because; "God is a spirit: and they that worship him must worship him in spirit and in truth" (Jn 4:24).

Are We There Yet?

The word "there" suggests a place. When do we stop? We don't! Ministry is 24/7. Even in our death someone could come to the funeral and turn their life over to God. When we arrive in our ministry or purpose, true life begins. If you need to take the high road or the low road God is with you. When starting a trip, there are some preparations to be put in order. Either you're going to bring food or get some on the way. Of course pit stops are on the way. Maybe you need to rest, stretch, or take restroom breaks. These days a GPS device is giving you directions. When you miss a turn or exit, the device tells you to make a U-turn or it reroutes. These procedures are to get you there in a timely manner. The rerouting means you were going your own way or you slipped up. The U-turn means the same. It will also say that "this is the shortest route" or whether or not a toll is ahead. Never-the-less you get there.

Is Jesus rerouting you or instructing you to do a U-turn?

_____
_____
_____
_____

Are you at the place where you realize that the fight is principality based and your weapon is obedience.? Are you at the place where you know that your position just requires you to stand firm in Him? Are you aware of the persons put in your way that are trials and tests that you must past to get to the next level?

_____
_____
_____
_____
_____
_____
_____
_____
_____
_____
_____
_____

Skipping Steps

When stepping correctly it feels like strides in purpose. You did as Jesus directed 1, 2, 3, 4,… not 1, 3, 7… As babes in Christ it is very important that every detail is in order. He deals in order and not confusion. Repeating steps can bruise ministry or refine a ministry. On the outside it looks fine but Jesus sees the internal bleeding. Following directions is detrimental in kingdom building. Its like you crawl to walk to run. You can also say that when learning to speak you annunciate the letters correctly so you'll be better under- stood when communicating to others.

I was in a rush for... and I realized...

_____
_____
_____
_____

Order my steps in thy word: and let not any iniquity have dominion over me (Ps 119-133)

During those times when we tried to rush Jesus. He showed us patience and faith. His plan is not to slow you up or condemn you. He is intentional and perfect. He molds us to adjust to the life He wants us to lead. When trials come we are assured that the potter has formed this clay to withstand the tricks of the enemy. Yes, we slip-up! This flesh cannot be tamed without the Holy Ghost. There have been those who tried but "… when I would do good, evil is present with me" (Romans 7:21). Don't skip the steps unless you're ordained and directed to by the Lord, because words like "suddenly" and "now" are without process!

In this particular situation following God's direction caused a major difference in my life when I didn't skip steps because...

_____
_____
_____
_____

Don't trip!

Against All Odds

Society said you wouldn't make it and you would not get far. You've surpassed the norm and have been ordained in your assignment. He holds tomorrow.

They said you wouldn't walk and now you run miles. They said you could not communicate. Now you speak, laugh, and smile. They figured you'd be lonely because of your past lifestyle. Now your marriage is ten years deep and you're now carrying another child.

They said your Prophetess status was just for profit. Actually they're incorrect, and speaking out of turn and your ministry is an asset to the kingdom, "You are Jesus legit," and you pray for their spiritual mindsets.

The doctors say you only have six months and that's stretching it. It has been four years since that statement and you are approaching five years because in Jesus name you declared life. Your lawyer says that you will do time and there is nothing he can do. The Judge bangs the gavel saying this case is dismissed and where are your accusers?

The bank said in two months your house will be in foreclosure so you dropped and prayed to God! Your address is still the same and they are shaking their heads in wonder. You can't afford a new car because of you financial status. Now you got a raise three days later and your check proves you can handle it.

The surgeon says on the first test it looks like there's bleeding on the brain. You are aware of your assignment and right now, in faith, death is not a part of it. The second test is not the same. Your son won't make it; and he's in a coma. Two weeks later, He woke up singing "How I Made It Over."

Thank you, Jesus, for operating in your own time, because against all odds we were delivered and You were glorified. Ponder this:

Many are the afflictions of the righteous but the Lord delivered them out of them all (Ps 34:19)

What has Jesus done for you that the world said couldn't be done?

_____
_____
_____
_____

Isn't Jesus Amazing!

Flammable

Is your soul treated to be susceptible to the fire laid upon us as cloven tongues? Is your soul untreated and suspected to be in the lake of fire? Let's be clear the first state, non-flammable, suggest eternal life and being fireproof. The second state suggests an eternal death of burning without being consumed. This word flammable can also be spread by the good news for glorification or bad news if you are just self-edifying with no cover. Being a child of God your flame should be shown at all times. Fire is also used as a sterilization. Our sin sick souls can be sterilize by this fire, the Holy Ghost fire. My daughter, Danielle Whitehead, and I collaborated on a song called "I Got That Fire." Some verses ask questions about the fire; "What is this fire that does not consume the bush that told Moses to take off his shoes." The word fire is used in different ways and aspects in the Bible.

And of the angels he saith, Who maketh his angels spirits, and his ministers a flame of fire (Heb 1:7)

How has the "Fire" been applied in your life?

_____
_____
_____
_____
_____
_____
_____
_____
_____
_____
_____
_____

This title, "Flammable," does not require much. Either you are or you're not. It's been suggested that there is a between but, fence straddle's may fall by the wayside.

Live

Can these bones live? Can this flesh hold pain? Can the spirit live amongst it and what's to gain? Yes, Jesus conquered Calvary. All hail to Jesus name!

Can this tongue be tamed? Can it just speak life? Can the teeth be spared the gnashing of an eternal flame? Yes, as the word cuts like a double-sided blade and it produces life!

Can these limbs adjust? Can they be subdued? Can they be used as Jesus' utensils? Can they move when He says move? Yes, the Holy Ghost will take over and override this wretchedness. Yes, He's omnipotent, omniscient, and omnipresent.

Can the blood purify? Can the mind abstain? Can the rituals be called out? Can praise and worship take its place? Yes, Christ shook off death. We will be raptured up and shaking lose this earthly frame.

Can my movement be staggered when facing the fork in the road? Jesus said, "No, my sheep hear my voice." They've adjusted to only hearing my tone.

Again he said unto me, Prophesy upon these bones, and say unto them, O ye dry bones, hear the word of the Lord (Ezek 37:4)

What are your thoughts concerning dry bones?

_____
_____
_____
_____
_____
_____
_____
_____
_____
_____
_____
_____
_____
_____
_____
_____
_____
_____

The Message You Heard vs. The Message You Speak

Being in church for a lifetime serves no purpose if you have no relationship with Jesus. Going to church just for certain services, holidays, problems, or for a need is not enough. You've heard the preachers say, change your ways; Jesus is the key; Love your neighbor; prayer changes things; read you Bible; fast and pray; you are your brother's keeper; Jesus is coming like a thief in the night; Every knee shall bow… and thank him for his mercy and grace.

Yet we as Christians still say "good luck," "just so happened," and "by chance." A good Samaritan isn't always recognized as much as a fighter or murder. An animal rescue is widely publicized, but Jesus saving a life or turning someone's life around is only recognized at your local church, maybe. Predators, prostitutes, perpetrators, liars, thieves, thugs, addicts, and murderers can be and are saved. There are no perfect people in church. There may be some that forgot where they came from! Their past reputations are still fresh in our minds and on our lips. Which isn't right! Bullies, backstabbers, and back bitters have caused cold and civil wars. Unrest seems to be normal. The judgments and stigmas people face are disheartening. Individuals with diseases and illnesses are met with, "that's what you get" and "what did you do."

Having the mind of Christ is a successful tool in everyday life. I have tried to wrap my mind around those who forget that they were sinners and being judgmental. Why call yourselves past names after you have taken up your bed and walked? That is not the name on Jesus' roll.

Just reflect on where God has brought you from. There is more space in the back! Then remember this verse:

So when they continued asking him, he lifted up himself, and said unto them, He that is without sin among you, let him first cast a stone at her (Jn 8:7)

I was a/an_____ Now I am_____
I was a/an_____ Now I am_____
I was a/an_____ Now I am_____

"You read that Jesus says love everybody but you speak hatred." (1 Jn 4:7-8).

"Treating people the way you feel like treating them is not His way" (Lk 6:31).

"Counting out the young people as if they are not our future" (Acts 2:17).

"Not paying people what they are worth" (Lk 10:7).

Do You See What He Said?

As Christians the belief of an immaculate conception, the death and resurrection is crucial. The father, Son and Holy Ghost is difficult to understand by most! This section asks about your belief. In Genesis, when Adam and Eve were put out of the Garden of Eden all that He said come to past. The disconnection wasn't repaired until Jesus. When God promised that the world would no more be destroyed by water, He sent a rainbow as a covenant. After the rains a rainbow is a reminder till this day. (You see what He said). Your faith is important and detrimental to the praise and worship of Christ. Your purpose is seasonal. A physical death is imminent and a spiritual death is true for an incomplete assignment.

When did you see what He said?

_____
_____
_____
_____

And God said, Let the waters under the heaven be gathered together unto one place, and let the dry land appear: and it was so (Gen 1:9) (You've seen, what He said.).

I said, Lord, be merciful unto me: heal my soul; for I have sinned against thee (Ps 41:4) (You've seen, what He said.).

When I said, My foot slippeth; thy mercy, O Lord, held me up (Ps 94:18) (You've seen, what He said.).

It was meet that we should make merry, and be glad: for this thy brother was dead, and is alive again; and was lost, and is found (Lk 15:32) (You've seen, what He said).

How do these verses pertain to your life?

_____
_____
_____
_____

People! He's trying to make "contact!"

Disclaimers Disclosures, Dishonest

Disclaimers -Disown your past. Jesus has washed away your sins because you asked. Everything is gone, diminished, and absent forever. Example: (Lk 15).

Disclosures —Bring to light all your burdens. Lay them down. "Is your all on the alter? You cannot heal what you don't say. Testify, because they were healed by their testimonies. Example: (Jn 4).

Dishonest - Sin is not trustworthy; it cheats, it's conniving, it's brutal, it's uncomfortable, it's not cute, it festers, and it can hurt. Example: (Gen'3).

Can you write down the instances in your life that Disclaimers, Disclosures and Dishonesty was in your life? A "thank you Jesus" must proceed after this!

_____
_____
_____
_____
_____
_____
_____
_____
_____
_____
_____
_____
_____

Being able to face yourself is a good thing. Admitting that you were once bound and now deliverance and freedom reside in you, falls right in line with redemption. Now, Walk your talk!

Amen Corners

Cliques, clubs, support groups, and meet-ups are nice arenas if they do what they're meant to do. You can kind of expect what you need from each one. They all deal with hopeful relationships. Do you expect the same results when there is a change/shift in your ministry, life, job, or family? If you do, you are probably "...amongst men most miserable." If not I applaud you, (but not praise you). Persons, places, and things are seasonal. It's just the way it is. In and during growth, things come off, come on, and fall out of place. If you are determined to stay in or with the save environment, you may be stunting your growth. As we grow from child to adult, your corners should either change or expand. While we are on the subject, "Yes men" can only go but so far. At some time or another, the truth needs to be told, shared, or confronted by you.

When you finally recognize your "Amen Corner" are they helping or hindering? Change is letting go to receive!

_____
_____
_____
_____

That we henceforth be no more children, tossed to and fro, and carried about with every wind of doctrine, by the sleight of men, and cunning craftiness, whereby they lie in wait to deceive. (Eph 4:14)

I urge you to make sure your foundation is sure and true. There are so many false five-fold-ministry leaders and others. They will conceal themselves until they see a way clear to persuade, distract, and mess you up if you don't know, that you know, that you know. Your "amen corner" should consist of spiritually intelligent folks, those with a fraternal spirit, and acts on a 24/7 ministry period. Looking alike is not a requirement (...some through the fire and some through the flood...). The goal of a well done and a kingdom building mindset is necessary.

_____
_____
_____
_____

Surround yourself with positive influences and not with those who can ruin it

_____

Check Your Punctuation Marks

Do you know; when to question, when to stop, when to pause, when to speak, when to listen, when to get excited, and when not to speak? If we paid more attention to Jesus, things would work out better. If something isn't right, stop it, period. When you say that Jesus told you something, make sure that you are supposed to tell someone else. It's okay to question others, but gossip has no place in kingdom building. When Jesus blesses you financially, spiritually, or physically, sharing can be spiritually dangerous. Everyone is not happy for you. Some do not want you to excel beyond them. Write a three- or five-year plan. Make a list. "Write the vision…" (Hab 2:2). Being still in ministry is not a bad thing. Jesus is working things out and you may need working on. Pause, you weapon is obedience. Until the Lord opens the door, praise him in the hallway! I'm always excited about Jesus. He always shows up, to show out, while shutting down man's agenda. Sit back and watch Him work it out.

I can apply punctuation marks during my everyday purpose because…

_____
_____
_____
_____

This was a moment to pause. *"And he took bread, and gave thanks, and brake it, and gave unto them, saying, This is my body which is given for you: this do in remembrance of me."* (Lk 22:19).

This was a moment to stop. *"So when they continued asking him, he lifted up himself, and said unto them, He that is without sin among you, let him first cast a stone at her"* (Jn 8:7).

This was a question? *"And the Lord said unto Satan, Whence comest thou? Then Satan answered the Lord, and said, From going to and fro in the earth, and from walking up and down in it"* (Job 1:7)

Too Much talking. *"And Joseph dreamed a dream, and he told it his brethren: and they hated him yet the more"* (Gen 37:5).

Make a list. *"Saying, I am Alpha and Omega, the first and the last: and, What thou seest, write in a book, and send it unto the seven churches which are in Asia; unto Ephesus, and unto Smyrna, and unto Pergamos, and unto Thyatira, and unto Sardis, and unto Philadelphia, and unto Laodicea"* (Rev 1:11).

Showing feelings(!) *"Saying, Father, if thou be willing, remove this cup from me: nevertheless not my will, but thine, be done" (Lk 22:42).*

Since Jesus is intentional there should be more spiritual control, which is more of Him, and less emotional control, which is us.

Who Are You?

Who are you? Are you wearing a false face? I see you dressed up, but I'm discerning that your intentions are out of place. Who are you really when you pray and bow your head? I sense confusion in you. Hello, can you hear me? Is there anybody in there? Who are you really and are you absolutely clear? Can you recognize the reflection in the mirror? Who are you really? Can you say praise the Lord? Can you continue to bless Him in your community, on the job, and at home?

Who are you really? Are you just captivated by the choir and dancers? Are you thirsty for the word? Are you asking questions and getting answers? Do others know who you are and are you promoting unity? Are you speaking life and praising God? Are you too busy gossiping? Can you cope in your midnights, that third watch just before dawn? Do you just pray during your day? Hello? Do you know what's going on? Can you ignore the distractions? Can you filter out the mess? Can you come out from among them and stop feeding the stress?

Are you? Can you? Will you? Do you? Yes, should come through as you quote "I can do all things through Christ…" (Phil 4:13) and "greater is He that is inside of you…" (1 Jn 4:4)

Are You prepared? Every day that you wake up, gives you another chance to get it right! Please, make good use of your time! Write out the consequences. It will encourage you to do better!

When I don't make good use of my time this happens!

_____
_____
_____
_____

Preparation! Preparation! Preparation!

Accountability

If you are unaware that you are your brother's keeper; Then now you know that you are your brother's keeper. Faith leaders, sanctuary folks, stay at home church folks, and everyone, accountability is a sure thing. Leading one astray just to edify yourself is not the way. Yes, Jesus has washed our sins away. Yes, you are saved from past sins. Yes, there are consequences, but grace and mercy are still in place, but only for a season. Jesus will keep you amidst your inconsistencies. The devil thought that old life style of sin was going to kill you or keep you astray. Now, you stand upon them using it as a footstool, a testimony, a reason to live, and a reason to let others know to look and live.

Past Accountability	Grace & Mercy
Unwed Parent	Those children kept you off the streets, because you were focused on caring for them. Now you're a wife. NOW, you're a **Missionary**
Drug dealer	You served time in Prison, since the streets weren't kind and your life was spared in jail. NOW, you're **Preacher**
Prostitute	Yes, your body was used up and beat up, but after Jesus you're a wife and mother. NOW, you're a **Pastor**
Adulterer	Now, you have your own family. NOW, you're an **Evangelist**
Thief	Now, you have your own Mechanic Shop. NOW, you're a **Deacon.**
Drug Addict	Now you're delivered and spreading the gospel. You've been letting people know the difference between an addict and beingdelivered.
Rebellious	NOW, you're a **Prophet**
Just Counted out	NOW, you're an **Apostle.**

I was a

_____
_____
_____
_____

But now I'm

_____
_____
_____
_____

"Watch ye therefore, and pray always, that ye may be accounted worthy to escape all these things that shall come to pass, and to stand before the before the Son of man."

Pro's and Con's

CON'S WITHOUT JESUS	PRO'S WITH JESUS
Feeling worthless and low self-esteem.	"I will praise thee; for I am fearfully and wonderfully made: marvelous are thy works; and that my soul knoweth right well" (Ps 139:14)
To many chaotic thoughts and can't seem to focus.	"Thou wilt keep him in perfect peace, whose mind is stayed on thee: because he trusteth in thee" (Isa 26:3).
Don't know who to love and where love is	"Beloved, let us love one another: for love is of God; and everyone that loveth is born of God, and knoweth God" (1 Jn 4:7).
My patience is running thin.	"Wait on the Lord: be of good courage, and he shall strengthen thine heart: wait, I say, on the Lord" (Ps 27:14).
The more I run around the less I get done.	"Be still, and know that I am God: I will be exalted among the heathen, I will be exalted in the earth" (Ps 46:10).
My haters and enemies are wearing me down.	"The Lord said unto my Lord, Sit thou at my right hand, until I make thine enemies thy footstool" (Ps 110:1)
I need this and I need that and low on cash.	"But my God shall supply all your needs according to his riches in glory by Christ Jesus" (Phil 4:19).
I often feel taken advantage of	"Blessed are the meek: for they shall inherit the earth" (Matt 5:5).

In all thy ways acknowledge him, and he shall direct thy paths (Proverbs 3:6)

What was your Con & Pro?

_____
_____
_____

*Making moves without seeking God is "Cautionary Proc*edures

ADDITIONAL NOTES

ADDITIONAL NOTES

ADDITIONAL NOTES

ADDITIONAL NOTES

ADDITIONAL NOTES

ADDITIONAL NOTES

ADDITIONAL NOTES

ADDITIONAL NOTES

ADDITIONAL NOTES

ADDITIONAL NOTES

ADDITIONAL NOTES

ADDITIONAL NOTES

ADDITIONAL NOTES

ADDITIONAL NOTES

ADDITIONAL NOTES

ADDITIONAL NOTES

ADDITIONAL NOTES

ADDITIONAL NOTES

ADDITIONAL NOTES

ADDITIONAL NOTES

ADDITIONAL NOTES

ADDITIONAL NOTES

ADDITIONAL NOTES

ADDITIONAL NOTES

ADDITIONAL NOTES

ADDITIONAL NOTES

ADDITIONAL NOTES

ADDITIONAL NOTES

ADDITIONAL NOTES

ADDITIONAL NOTES

ADDITIONAL NOTES

ADDITIONAL NOTES

ADDITIONAL NOTES

ADDITIONAL NOTES

ADDITIONAL NOTES

ADDITIONAL NOTES

ADDITIONAL NOTES

ADDITIONAL NOTES

ADDITIONAL NOTES

www.ingramcontent.com/pod-product-compliance
Lightning Source LLC
Chambersburg PA
CBHW051806100526
44592CB00016B/2585